Monkey Chinese Horoscope 2023

By
IChingHun FengShuisu

Table of Contents

Introduce 5

Year of the MONKEY (Wood) | (1944) & (2004)....................8

    Overview 8

    Career and Business 9

    Financial 10

    Family.. 11

    Love... 12

    Health 12

Year of the MONKEY (Fire) | (1956) & (2016)..................... 13

    Overview 13

    Career and Business 15

    Financial 16

    Family... 18

    Love... 18

    Health 19

Year of the MONKEY (Fire) | (1968) 20

    Overview 20

    Career and Business 21

    Financial 22

    Family... 23

    Love... 24

    Health 25

Year of the MONKEY (Earth) | (1980) 26

    Overview 26

    Career and Business 27

    Financial 28

    Family... 29

Love 30

Health 31

Year of the MONKEY (Water) | (1992) 32

Overview 32

Career and Business 33

Financial 34

Family 35

Love 36

Health 37

Chinese Astrology Horoscope for Each Month 38

Month 12 in the Tiger Year (6 Jan 23 - 3 Feb 23) 38

Month 1 in the Rabbit Year (4 Feb 23 - 5 Mar 23) 41

Month 2 in the Rabbit Year (6 Mar 23 - 5 Apr 23) 43

Month 3 in the Rabbit Year (6 Apr 23 - 5 May 23) 45

Month 4 in the Rabbit Year (6 May 23 - 5 Jun 23) 47

Month 5 in the Rabbit Year (6 Jun 23 - 6 Jul 23) 49

Month 6 in the Rabbit Year (7 Jul 23 - 7 Aug 23) 51

Month 7 in the Rabbit Year (8 Aug 23 - 7 Sep 23) 53

Month 8 in the Rabbit Year (8 Sep 23 - 7 Oct 23) 55

Month 9 in the Rabbit Year (8 Oct 23 - 6 Nov 23) 57

Month 10 in the Rabbit Year (7 Nov 23 - 6 Dec 23) 59

Month 11 in the Rabbit Year (7 Dec 23 - 5 Jan 24) 61

Amulet for The Year of the Monkey 64

The character of people born in the year of the MONKEY

People born this year have smart, cunning personality that is hidden behind cuteness. They talk because they are cute, they are fun-loving, they have intelligence that is easy to teach, and they can learn quickly. People born in this year are very attractive and charming. They are usually very interested in social gatherings. However, they rarely hide their own emotions because everything will come out on their faces as they get to know each other. People born in this year are excellent problem solvers. If you have a problem, they will always offer to assist you, will be a good listeners, and will always suggest the appropriate words. Curiosity drives people born this year to constantly learn. The disadvantage of the Year of the Monkey is that there is sometimes a lack of reason. And you're ready to paint a picture for yourself and others to believe in everything people born in the Year of the Monkey do. Staying is always the best option. People born in the Year of the Monkey are perceived as selfish, opportunistic, and cunning by some. People born in this year are uninterested. Friends born in this year are devoted and loyal. Aside from that, you're a sweet-tempered but repulsive lover who fades quickly.

Strength:
You value unity and enjoy resolving problems for others.

Weaknesses:
You enjoy teasing others, and as a result, you are looked down upon; don't think twice before acting.

Love:
People born this year have a lot of love because they are cute, talkative, and talkative. In addition to extramarital affairs, they frequently manage their charms when they like someone and get to know each other without hesitation. People born this year as boyfriends look cute because they are calm, always consider the feelings of others, don't like to fuss, frequently

talk to each other for a reason, and if they still don't agree with someone, they will ask to be together for a long time. proof but if you find the person who likes you the most, just getting along with each other is enough.

Suitable Career:
People born in the Year of the Monkey are thought to be of the golden element. Architects, actors, artists, handicrafts, brokers, consultants, banks, and opening a shop selling construction materials are all professions that promote and suit your destiny. Working in metallurgy, machinery, selling automobiles or automobile accessories, iron ore, industrial plants, ceramics, selling jewelry, or even agricultural work Real estate development is a lucrative business for people born in the year of the Monkey.

Year of the MONKEY (Wood) | (1944) & (2004)

"The Monkey eats the fruit" is a person born in the year of the MONKEY at the age of 79 years (1944) and 19 years (2004)

Overview

Even if the planet orbiting into your destiny house this year is the "lawsuit star," auspicious stars are orbiting to support you in your lifetime, causing you to receive auspicious power to visit. The work will be completed in a year. The trade business will grow. There will be an opportunity to open a branch or a new store, as well as a criterion for purchasing expensive assets in the house. It is quite promising in terms of investment direction. Furthermore, this year is regarded as favorable. that you will pass on your experience to your heirs or grandchildren for them to participate in an internship Prepare to take over the work to take care of the business. However, due to the villain's influence, the lawsuit aiming to harass must be cautious of the minor cause causing trouble, causing you to go in and fix it. If you are under a lot of stress this year. Inviting him to pray and pay respect to monks will help to lighten his load.

The planet orbiting this year's destiny for the young destiny around the age of 19 is "Humty Star." This year's research will be forward-thinking. However, you should always strive to improve yourself to keep up with current events. This year, be cautious of accidents while participating in sports or driving. Also, be cautious because there will be water hazards. Therefore, if traveling by water, you should be more careful.

Career and Business

This year's education career will find a way to progress, with the possibility of opening more branches or expanding. External investment is encouraged, particularly during the month when the prince's career and education are both flourishing.: 2nd month of China (6 Mar.-4 Apr.), 3rd month of China (5 Apr.-5. May), the 7th month of China (8 Aug. - 7 Sep.) and the 11th month of China (7 Dec 22 - 5 Jan 23), however, you should exercise caution throughout the year. Some people are attacking, accusing, and possibly causing a legal dispute. The fate of both ages must be watched carefully, especially during the months that are not favorable, namely the 1st month of China (4 Feb. – 5 Mar.), the 4th month of China (6 May. – 5 Jun.), the 9th month of China (8 Oct. – 6 Nov.) and 10th month of China (7 Nov. – 6 Dec.) are concerned about being accused of being involved in a lawsuit As a result, you should be cautious with your words and actions to avoid problems in the long run.

Financial

This year's financial fortunes will be abundant income and cash inflows from both directions, but there will also be expenses in long lines of waiting. As a result, even if it is a costly asset purchase or a business investment, however, if the budget is exceeded, there will be a lack of liquidity. As a result, you should have a backup plan or good management in place. Especially during the month when your financial star is down and you need to closely monitor your income and expenses, such as the 1st month of China (4 Feb. - 5 Mar.), the 4th month of China (6 May - 5 Jun)., in the 9th month of China (8

Oct. - 6 Nov.) and in the 10th month of China (7 Nov. - 6 Dec.), preventing others from borrowing money or signing guarantees. Do not take chances with your luck. Avoid investing in illegal enterprises. For months with good financial liquidity, namely, the 2nd month of China (6 Mar. – 4 Apr.), 3rd month of China (5 Apr. – 5 May), 7th month of China (8 Aug. – 7 Sep.), and 11th month of China (7 Dec. 22 – 5 Jan. 23).

Family

This year's fortunes are not looking good for the family; avoid squabbles with neighbors. As a result, you must be able to control your emotions. Don't be too harsh or arrogant. Otherwise, a minor issue may escalate into a major one that will not be easily resolved. Especially during the months when families are prone to turmoil, conflicts easily include the 1st month of China (4 Feb. – 5 Mar.), the 4th month of China (6 May – 5 Jun.), the 9th month of China (8 Oct. – 6 Nov.) and the 10th month of China (7 Nov. – 6 Dec.). At such times, you should avoid extending the length of the woman and be cautious of safety and people's health around the house.

Love

Even for the elderly, this year's love horoscope is in the middle range, but your heart and needs are still full. Even if the beep can be kicked loudly, you should be cautious because you may become engulfed in a love disease that will humiliate your children. Therefore, it must be adjusted to suit this age. By the month you need to be careful of love, there will be fragile problems,1st month of China (4 Feb. - 5 Mar.), 4th month of China (6 May. - 5 Jun.), 9th month of China (8 Oct. – 6 Nov.) and 10th month, China (7 Nov. – 6 Dec.) where you should avoid going to entertainment venues.

Health

This year's destiny is not in good health; you should rest more. Choose foods that are both nutritious and easy to digest. Spicy foods and meat are difficult to digest and harmful to your health. As a result, Elder should look after his own physical and mental health. By the month of the destiny's body, both age cycles are easy to get sick, including 1st month of China (4 Feb. - 5 Mar.), 4th month of China (6 May - 5 Jun.), 9th month of China (8 Oct. – 6 Nov.) and 10th month of China (7 Nov. – 6 Dec.).

Year of the MONKEY (Fire) | (1956) & (2016)

"The MONKEY in a herd" is a person born in the year of the MONKEY at the age of 67 years (1956) and 7 years (2016)

Overview

Because the planet circling your fate this year is "Hum Tee Bad Star." This year, various works will be completed. You must exercise caution. Every possible activity cannot be impatient. Investment decisions, in particular, must be carefully considered; do not simply hear that there is a profit and rush to invest. Because it could be a one-time profit. There may be a loss until there is nothing left in the future because many bad stars are aiming at you this year. In addition to the evil star "Hum Ti," "Star Ngwe Sua" (Planet Moon) and "Puehua Star" (Flying

Star) are on their way to destruction. As a result, money is extremely important. Do not allow leak points to cause unnecessary waste of money. In the workplace, you should always strive to maintain positive relationships with those you must deal with. Partners, customers, supervisors, and associates are all included. Another important factor to consider is health issues. Keep an eye out for headaches and stomach pains; while they may not appear to be serious, they could be a sign of an emerging silent disorder. As a result, you should be aware of any abnormalities in your body and should have annual checkups. Furthermore, liquor and all other evil things should be avoided. Because it may result in job failure and financial loss. One should avoid nightlife at entertainment venues in particular because, in addition to causing unemployment and low income, it also causes endless problems for the family.

Dao Jui is the planet orbiting this year's destiny house for a 7-year-old child. This is due to an imbalance between the water and earth elements, resulting in annihilation. When going out with a child this age, an adult should be cautious of straying. To be hygienic, the cleanliness of food should be emphasized, including various external infectious diseases, both airborne diseases, and diarrhea.

Career and Business

This year, destiny's trade operations are prone to errors. Commercial investments are also vulnerable to deception or fraud. As a result, before investing, the person and other factors should be thoroughly reviewed. Because joining and investing this year is fraught with danger. Profitability becomes less likely as a result. a variety of investments You must exercise extreme caution if it is unavoidable after investing. You should also check in regularly. Another critical issue that must be addressed is communication. External contacts deal with partners and customers, while internal contacts deal with subordinates or people at a higher level. To avoid decision-making mistakes, communication should be clear. Make no decisions because you are provoked or flattered. Also, don't let emotion take precedence over logic. In particular, if entering the following months when trade and work will encounter problems and obstacles, namely the 1st month of China (4 Feb. – 5 Mar.), the 4th month of China (6 May – 5 Jun.) In the 9th month of China (8 Oct. – 6 Nov.) and in the 10th month of China (7 Nov. – 6 Dec.), Be cautious when investing because you will be duped and there will be conflicts between the parties. The contract will be met with special terms that benefit. You should also be wary of accounting fraud. For the month that the work is bright and smooth, such as the 2nd month of China (6 Mar. - 4 Apr.), the 3rd month of China (5 Apr. - 5 May.), the 7th month of China (8 Aug. – 7 Sep.) and 11th month of China (7 Dec. 22 – 5 Jan. 23).

Financial

This year's fortunes, finances, and chances of change are favorable. When it comes to fortune money, there must be a reason to go out frequently. Giving you a moment's joy is what it's called. However, if you are still extremely greedy, you have the right to influence the money in your pocket, causing the liquidity to shrink. There is also a criterion for losing a large sum of money in an unexpected circumstance. Especially during the months in which the financial hardships occur, namely, 1st month of China (4 Feb. – 5 Mar.), China 4th month of China (6 May – 5 Jun), 9th month of China (8 Oct. – 6 Nov.) and the 10th month of China (7 Nov. – 6 Dec.) where you prohibit others from borrowing money and signing guarantees Avoid gambling on speculation. Do not engage in any illegal or immoral business that could lead to a lawsuit. Be wary of incorrect accounting or fraud, which can cost you money and incur large expenses, causing your liquidity to deteriorate. And if you invest during that time, be wary of being duped. As for the months in which the financial liquidity flows smoothly, they are 2nd month of China (6 Mar. - 4 Apr.), 3rd month of China (5 Apr. - 5 May.), 7th month of China (8 Aug. – 7 Sep.) and the 11th month of China (7 Dec. 22 – 5 Jan. 23), however, you should not underestimate. Always know how to plan your expenses. To prevent working capital lack of liquidity.

Family

The evil constellation aimed at the family base disrupted the family's peace this year. As a result, you should be aware of household accidents and illnesses. Including arguments and quarrels, especially during the months in which the family will experience chaos, such as the 1st month of China (4 Feb. - 5 Mar.), the 4th month of China (6 May - 5 Jun)., the 9th month of China (8 Oct. - 6 Nov.) and in the 10th month of China (7 Nov. - 6 Dec.), which should result in increased safety precautions. Because even if it happened only once. However, it may result in a loss and a lot of trouble for you. As a result, do not be careless and be aware that you may be slandered, assaulted, or charged with a crime.

Love

Even if your love horoscope is good this year, your partner or opposite sex will look after you. But, even in your old age, there will be a third party to break up with you. But the heart is still throbbing with life, a hundred loves and losses just a few inches apart. As a result, be careful not to become obsessed with people outside the home to the point of abandoning your partner. Especially during the 1st month of China (4 Feb. – 5 Mar.), 4th month of China (6 May – 5 Jun.), 9th month of China (8 Oct. – 6 Nov.)) and the 10th month of China (7 Nov – 6 Dec) where you should avoid going to entertainment venues. Because, in addition to providing the opportunity to become infected by being duped into losing money, it also destroys family love and peace.

Health

The health horoscope for this year is bleak. It's because the evil stars Nguy Shuang and Puehua have infiltrated the house of fate. As a result, you should exercise caution when working and traveling. Especially during the months that you should pay special attention to health care, such as the 1st month of China (4 Feb. - 5 Mar.), the 4th month of China (6 May - 5 June), 9th month of China (8 Oct. – 6 Nov.) and the 10th month of China (7 Nov. – 6 Dec.) must be cautious of alcohol's dangers. Don't drink more than you need to. Also, be wary of work that does not allow for adequate rest or health checks. Fat can clog arteries and cause major problems. They must also be cautious of unexpected road accidents. This includes being cautious of infectious diseases from eating whatever you want. Be cautious of high blood pressure and other hidden diseases.

Year of the MONKEY (Fire) | (1968)

" The Monkey love in the Freedom " is a person born in the year of the MONKEY at the age of 55 years (1968)

Overview

Although the planet that orbits your destiny this year is "Star Guo Hu" (lawsuit star), you have the power of the good star that supports and encourages you to have friends. And the people around you are very supportive of your various activities; this year is a year of opportunity. For some, you will have the opportunity to reclaim ownership of the company. You will have a channel through which to expand trade. Those who are still working full-time or in government service will have to wait a year for results. Because you will be supported by adults, there is a chance for advancement. But be careful, speaking and sly friends will put you in danger. However, there is auspicious power to visit the house this year for the family. An auspicious event may occur. Moving into a new home is auspicious. It is regarded as a lucky year. However, there are evil stars that invade the house of fate throughout the year, so avoid conflicts, arguments, and litigation from conflicts that will drag you into involvement. As a result, individual ability plays a role in success. To transform the crisis into an opportunity for the Lord.

Career and Business

This year's business, including business, is prosperous and there is no cause for concern. Those who trade will have the opportunity to open new channels if they do not stop developing themselves, seeking knowledge of technology, and staying current with the situation. Those who work full-time will receive special attention from their boss. Colleagues and subordinates will also offer assistance. You have the criteria to be promoted and promoted this year. Especially the month in which the stars of work are glorious, such as the 2nd month of China (6 Mar. – 4 Apr.), the 3rd month of China (5 Apr. – 5 May)), the 7th month of China (8 Aug. – 7 Sep) and the 11th month of China (7 Dec. 22 – 5 Jan.23), but if you enter the month that does not support you, which is the 1st month of China (4 Feb. – 5 Mar.) 4th month of China (6 May – 5 Jun.), 9th month of China (8 Oct. – 6 Nov.) and 10th month of China (7 Nov. – 6 Dec) You should avoid interfering in the affairs of others. Please do your best to carry out your responsibilities. Be wary of being duped when accepting any work. And maintain the relationship by not being arrogant, boasting, or arrogant; everything will pass.

Financial

This year's financial fortunes are abundant, with cash inflows from investments. There are opportunities for growth and investment. The overall investment will yield a positive return. Especially during the months when your finances are bright and smooth, such as the 2nd month of China (6 Mar. – 4 Apr.), the 3rd month of China (5 Apr. – 5 May), the 7th month of China (8 Aug. - 7 Sep.) and China's 11th month of China (7 Dec. 22 - 5 Jan.23). However, you should be aware of the following months when financial hardships occur: 1st month of China (4 Feb. – 5 Mar.), 4th month of China (6 May – 5 Jun.), 9th month of China (8 Oct. – 6 Nov.) and 10th month of China (7 Nov. – 6 Dec.) That should not be allowed to allow others to borrow money. And those who sign financial guarantees should avoid gambling and speculation. Avoid getting greedy and investing in illegal businesses or piracy. This is because there is a lawsuit aimed at the house this year, so there is a possibility of being sued. It's easier than in previous years, which will result in mental health and property losses. As a result, if you can avoid it, you should.

Family

The presence of auspicious power is responsible for this year's family horoscope. There is a criterion at home for auspicious work to occur. You will have the opportunity to purchase expensive assets or move into a new home at an auspicious time. However, the group will target many evil stars throughout the year. When entering the following month, destiny should be very careful of events and problems such as the 1st month of China (4 Feb. – 5 Mar.), the 4th month of China (6 May – 5 Jun.), the 9th month of China (8 Oct. – 6 Nov.) and the 10th month of China (7 Nov. – 6 Dec.) where you should be cautious about safety and accidents in your home It is hazardous due to the risk of falling from a great height as well as damaged equipment. They must be wary of brotherly feuds until there is a lawsuit that results in a court case. As a result, compromise should be sought. for the sake of the family's peace.

Love

This year has been difficult in terms of love. You and your spouse have a lot of disagreements. Furthermore, using sarcastic words to hurt the other person will leave a deep wound in the heart, leading to anger, and hatred, and easily causing divisions. If you can't control your emotions, this year's love may fall apart. Furthermore, be wary of third parties who will act as a catalyst to escalate the situation. Especially during the months when love is fragile and you should pay close attention, i.e. 1st month of China (4 Feb. – 5 Mar.), 4th month of China (6 May. – 5 Jun.), 9th month of China (8 Oct. – 6 Nov.) and 10th month of China (7 Nov. – 6 Dec.) Think before you speak in situations where you must make an extra effort to support your marriage. Do not meddle in other people's family matters. Avoid wandering around looking for services because you may become ill and cause arguments.

Health

Overall, your health is in good shape this year. However, the socialization that occurs frequently will cause problems. Drunkenness and lack of sleep are both harmful to your health and can impair your ability to work. As a result, if you consume alcohol, please refrain from operating machinery or driving. All of these hurt life and property. Especially during the months that you should not underestimate and should increase your care, such as the 1st month of china (4 Feb. – 5 Mar.), the 4th month of china (6 May. – 5 Jun.), the 9th month of china

(8 Oct. – 6 Nov.) and 10th month of china (7 Nov. – 6 Dec.) where you need to be extra careful because you might get into an accident or get caught. be in control.

Year of the MONKEY (Earth) | (1980)

" The Monkey is smart" is a person born in the year of the MONKEY at the age of 43 years (1980)

Overview

Even though the stars are squinting at the house of fate this year, it is also one of the auspicious years of destiny around this age. Work will bring you auspicious power in terms of building a more stable body. Many people will support the trade's direction. As a result, coupled with a constant desire to improve yourself to keep up with the environment, you will be able to achieve your goals and find success. Those who work full-time or go to government service will be accepted this year by their servants and colleagues. Both will have their work displayed and have received praise from adults. However, you should be aware that throughout the year, many evil stars will appear orbiting to focus and harass your mind, causing your mind to fluctuate up and down easily irritated. Unstable emotions and indecisive decisions frequently lead to arguments with those around you and the loss of assets. Although the overall trend is positive this year, you must choose the right time. It should be avoided during the 1st month of China (4 Feb. – 5 Mar.), the 4th month of China (6 May – 5 Jun.), the 9th month of China (8 Oct. – 6 Nov.), and the 10th month of China (7 Nov. – 6 Dec.) because there are criteria for fraudulent partners, employees to embezzle their assets or deceiving accounts causing damage.

Career and Business

Depending on your efforts, your work and business this year will be very fortunate. However, there are seasonal patterns and opportunities to expand trades throughout the year. So, whether you work full-time, are a government official, or own your own trading company. If you increase your enthusiasm this year, you will see good returns in your account.

The months in which your work is in a bright and prosperous direction are the 2nd month of China (6 Mar. – 4 Apr.), 3rd month of China (5 Apr. – 5 May), 7th month of China (8 Aug. – 7 Sep.) and 11th month of China (7 Dec. 22 – 5 Jan. .23) but if entering the following months that do not support you, i.e. 1st month of China (4 Feb. – 5 Mar.), 4th month of China (6 May. – 5 Jun.), the 9th month of China (8 Oct. – 6 Nov.) and in the 10th month of China (7 Nov. – 6 Dec.) where conflicts with colleagues or subordinates will cause problems. As a result, please focus on your work. Interfere with no one else's work.

Financial

This year's financial fortunes are looking up. However, with the income that occurs this year, you must invest heavily to lobby for the main will to have significant results. Especially during months when the financial stars are aligned, namely, 2nd month of China (6 Mar. - 4 Apr.), 3rd month of China (5 Apr. - 5 May.), 7th month of China (8 Aug. – 7 Sep.), and 11th month of China (7 Dec. 22 – 5 Jan. 23). However, there is a bad star this year. and the sluggish star that orbits and destroys as a result, despite the large inflow of income, unexpected expenditures, and financial leaks will occur, resulting in liquidity shortages. You should be especially cautious during the following months: 1st month of China (4 Feb. – 5 Mar.), 4th month of China (6 May – 5 Jun.), the 9th month of China (8 Oct. – 6 Nov.), and the 10th month of China (7 Nov. – 6 Dec.) You should not lend money or make guarantees, you should not be greedy, and you should avoid playing. Gambling and illegal business operations are both prohibited.

Family

This year, the house receives auspicious power from destiny. There will be an opportunity to welcome additional new members. Whether there is a requirement to purchase expensive real estate or to hold a merit-making ceremony for a new house or other auspicious events, the family members are overjoyed. But be careful during the months in which the family will encounter problems and chaos, such as the 1st month of China (4 Feb. – 5 Mar.), the 4th month of China (6 May. – 5 Jun.), the 9th month of

China. (8 Oct. – 6 Nov.) and the 10th month of China (7 Nov. – 6 Dec.) where there could be an extramarital affair. Unless there is a serious issue that requires a trip to the police station or a trip to court. Also, be cautious of misplaced valuables or robbed.

Love

This year, love for the destiny who is still single requires careful consideration because you will fall in love easily. But when you're in a relationship, you feel hesitant, as if you're not sure whether to say yes or no. So, instead of being stubborn, get together gradually and study for a long time. Go ahead if you feel close and confident. This year's love is frequently offended by those of you who are in love with a partner. There is an argument. You will use one example, while the other party will use the other. As a result, it would be necessary to give each other time to communicate to improve their understanding. If you don't control your emotions and cherish your love this year, problems will arise. Especially during the 1st month of China (4 Feb. – 5 Mar.), the 4th month of China (6 May – 5 Jun.), the 9th month of China

(8 Oct. – 6 Nov.), and the 10th month of China (7 Nov – 6 Dec). Be wary of escalating word-of-mouth.

Health

This year, your health horoscope is in the medium range, with a tendency to be low. It was because the health base was being harassed by a swarm of evil constellations. This will have an impact on life safety and health issues. As a result, both during travel and at work, accidents must be avoided. If the accumulated stress is not released, it can cause insomnia, headaches, and irritability, which can have serious consequences. The months you need to be careful of health problems are 1st month of China (4 Feb. – 5 Mar.), 4th month of China (6 May – 5 Jun.), the 9th month of China (8 Oct. – 6 Nov.), and the 10th month of China (7 Nov. – 6 Dec.) should make time to exercise regularly, even if any abnormalities are discovered. Should see a doctor right away for a diagnosis and treatment.

Year of the MONKEY (Water) | (1992)

" The monkey is climbing a tree." is a person born in the year of the MONKEY at the age of 31 years (1992)

Overview

Because the planet orbiting your destiny house this year is "Kao Hu" (lawsuit star) and the evil star "Ngw Sua" (Planet Moon) sends you around the age of 31, As a result, most people's lives are fraught with difficulties. Friends and family who cause trouble should be avoided. Furthermore, you must be wary of having problems with government agencies, illegal violations, copyright infringement, or contract breaches, and there are frequently conflicts and arguments with people around you. Destiny is a young girl who enjoys socializing with her friends. Take care not to avoid being punished by a criminal case. In terms of health, you should be wary of hidden diseases that may threaten you this year. And should exercise caution when driving a vehicle. But he is still fortunate that the auspicious star "Sue Ha" appeared during the year, orbiting to shine in the house of destiny, thus helping to drive away bad things and ease bad things from heavy to light. However, if you feel stressed at any point this year or exert pressure on things that affect prayer or going to make merit will help alleviate the negative effects.

Career and Business

This year is still in the knowledge-filling phase for the destiny of this age. To keep up with today's ever-changing circumstances, you should always strive to improve yourself. Listening to work study podcasts from a variety of people will increase your adaptability and flexibility in any situation. Please don't be distracted by useless things. Otherwise, someone else will be successful this year instead of you. Instead of grabbing liquid water, wasting work, and losing the future. You must be cautious, especially during the months when problems may arise. such as the 1st month of China (4 Feb. – 5 Mar.), the 4th month of China (6 May – 5 Jun.), the 9th month of China (8 Oct. – 6 Nov.), and the 10th month of China (7 Nov. – 6 Dec.) Please be cautious of being duped and suffering as a result of things you did not create but must endure. Without knowing the root cause, you became the accused in a lawsuit. Change jobs or have a better direction in the month in which your career and education direction has a better rhythm. Including smooth trading, including the 2nd month of China (6 Mar. – 4 Apr.), 3rd month of China (5 Apr. – 5 May.), 7th month of China (8 Aug. – 7 Sep.), and 11th month of China (7 Dec. 22 – 5 Jan. 23).

Financial

The matter of money and gold of destiny is regarded as mediocre this year. Even if you win the lottery, you will face unexpected expenses that will drain your savings. You should plan your money use early in the year, focusing on savings and researching additional investment channels. Don't mature and don't act like a big heart to your friends because it will only make things worse. It is critical this year to avoid an illegal business because a lawsuit will expedite your escape from punishment. So don't interfere and you'll be fine. Especially during the months when the financial stumbling block was the 1st month of China (4 Feb. – 5 Mar.), the

4th month of China (6 May – 5 Jun.), the 9th month of China (8 Oct. – 6 Nov.), and the 10th month of China (7 Nov. – 6 Dec.), where all activities must increase caution. Allow others to borrow money or sign guarantees on your behalf. Do not gamble, gamble, or be greedy for other people's wealth. For the months that are prosperous and bright, such as the 2nd month of China (6 Mar. – 4 Apr.), the 3rd month of China (5 Apr. – 5 May.), the 7th month of China (8 Aug. – 7 Sep.) and 11th month of China (7 Dec. 22 – 5 Jan. 23).

Family

The family will be in turmoil this year because the evil star is aiming for the family's base. As a result, you should be aware of any conflicts between members of the household and outsiders. Until it escalates and requires a police report or a lawsuit, there is something that cannot be overlooked, namely the health and safety of people in the home. Because you have a criterion to mourn your elder relatives this year, be wary of lost or stolen valuables. In particular, be especially careful during the following months: 1st month of China (4 Feb. –

5 Mar.), 4th month of China (6 May – 5 Jun.), the 9th month of China (8 Oct. – 6 Nov.), and the 10th month of China (7 Nov. – 6 Dec.) Beware of unexpected disasters with seniors living in the house during this period.

Love

The love horoscope of destiny as a whole is favorable. However, be wary of being attracted to the opposite sex as this will cause problems and trouble in the family. If you're still undecided this year, let's study as friends first to make everyone feel at ease. And avoid being alone with someone of the opposite sex. It's easy to crash if you let the atmosphere take you. Those who have a partner should be wary of the third hand interfering and causing the love to crack. Be wary of deviant behavior because it will lead to endless feuds. Especially jealousy events This year, the month that love will cause chaos and arguments will be easy: 1st month of China (4 Feb. - 5 Mar.), 4th month of China (6 May - 5 Jun)., 9th month of China (8 Oct. – 6 Nov.) and 10th month of China (7 Nov. – 6 Dec.).

Health

Your health horoscope around this age is not favorable. Because the evil stars "Hum Ti," "Dao Nguy Sua," and "Dao Puehua" are all in the group aiming for their health. You should therefore be cautious of latent diseases. And various infectious diseases will occur, including traveling or driving to avoid accidents. Especially during the months that you need to take extra care and take care of yourself, such as the 1st month of China (4 Feb. – 5 Mar.), the 4th month of China (6 May – 5 Jun.), the 9th month of China (8 Oct. – 6 Nov.) and 10th month of China (7 Nov. – 6 Dec.) where the destiny must not be careless. If intoxicated, avoid driving a vehicle.

Chinese Astrology Horoscope for Each Month

Month 12 in the Tiger Year (6 Jan 23 - 3 Feb 23)

Starting this year, the floor of your destiny that was born in the year of the Monkey is prosperous and bright, because there are auspicious stars in the lord's position in the zodiac, so you should seize this opportunity to work diligently. Since the beginning of the year, it has been a triumphant auspicious time. This time, your job duties, including business, will go as smoothly as you wish. Will be able to increase job opportunities or create new ones. Those who work full-time should work faster to produce results and make sales. Keep the numbers first so that you don't have too much trouble during the months when you don't have support.

The financial horoscope is dominant during this time. Money will flow both directly and indirectly. It will be earnings from a successful job or a good return on financial assistance. Furthermore, the fortune-teller has a criterion to invest in trading or purchasing larger assets, but you should balance your spending with your income. If you enjoy spending and ignoring your finances, you may also stumble and become stuck.

Cupid takes the side of love this month, and good things happen. that impresses each other, or you may be blessed by your lover When your luck improves, everything loosens up. The more diligent you are, the greater your rewards will be.

At this stage, health must pay attention to be cautious of working so hard that it causes insufficient rest, which has the potential to make you sick.

Cupid takes the side of love this month, and good things happen. that impresses each other, or you may be blessed by your lover When your luck improves, everything loosens up. The more diligent you are, the greater your rewards will be.

At this stage, health must be careful not to work so hard that it causes insufficient rest. has the authority to make you sick

Relatives and friends will be able to organize a worthy event or a charity event, or they will go on a long-distance trip together.

However, if the investment is poor, there is a risk of being duped. As a result, you should not invest or gamble.

Support Days: 2 Jan., 6 Jan., 10 Jan., 14 Jan., 18 Jan., 22 Jan., 26 Jan., 30 Jan.
Lucky Days: 11 Jan., 23 Jan.
Misfortune Days: 8 Jan., 20 Jan.
Bad Days: 5 Jan., 17 Jan., 29 Jan.

Month 1 in the Rabbit Year (4 Feb 23 - 5 Mar 23)
This month, your fate has shifted to the Chong border. As a result, life's journey is fraught with peril. Every activity requires extra caution and care.

You should do some things this month. Developing positive relationships in the chain of command at both the upper and lower levels. At the start of the year, you should have a clear direction and set goals to achieve your objectives, and you should prepare yourself to work hard. Interfere not with other people's responsibilities or any activities that will be carried out. You should be aware of this to avoid being easily knocked down.

This salary horoscope is not favorable. Don't just spend your money on cheap items. You must also follow the utilization principle. During this time, you should keep your working capital liquid. It should be a system that can be checked, including accounting work. Avoid gambling and gambling, and do not sign any guarantees. Do not be greedy for the property of others.

This month is not favorable for joint stocks and investments in various fields, and they should be postponed.

Family fate should be mindful of the safety and health of those in the home. Valuable possessions should be kept safely. Be cautious of salt as a worm, embezzlement, or theft.

In terms of love, it is a neutral criterion that is neither good nor bad.

Food cleanliness should be monitored for health reasons. Furthermore, be cautious of accidents while traveling.

Be wary of conflicts with relatives, friends, and friends like this.

Support Days: 3 Feb., 7 Feb., 11 Feb., 15 Feb., 19 Feb., 23 Feb., 27 Feb.
Lucky Days: 4 Feb., 16 Feb., 28 Feb.

Misfortune Days: 1 Feb., 13 Feb., 25 Feb.
Bad Days: 10 Feb., 22 Feb.

Month 2 in the Rabbit Year (6 Mar 23 - 5 Apr 23)
Chao Destiny's life path entered this month, receiving auspicious power to propel him forward. Work and sales should be picked up quickly and diligently to move forward.

There is one thing you should do during this time: beg you not to be proud of your achievements. However, you should always be humble so that you are not tempted by bullies.

There are still bright ways to expand business branches in terms of business, including business. Investing in raw materials is a good way to make money. In terms of other investments, there is a good portion.

This salary horoscope is favorable. Direct cash flows have been consistent. However, the fortune's funds will be lost. As a result, you should not be overly greedy and should not lend money or sign guarantees. Do not invest in companies that violate the law. Take care not to avoid punishment. They must also keep an eye on the leak. Be wary of accounting tampering or minors misappropriating funds.

Your family is at peace and free of conflicts.

The love story remains rosy and smooth. This month, your loved ones are especially attentive to you. As a result, it is a good time to discuss the accumulated issues to improve your understanding, or for those who are single and decide to use this period to confess their feelings, they are entitled to positive feedback.

If your health is adequate, you should seek medical attention as soon as possible.

Friends should avoid getting involved in conflicts between friends, especially when it comes to litigation. Take care not to be dragged.

Support Days: 3 Mar, 7 Mar., 11 Mar., 15 Mar., 19 Mar., 23 Mar., 27 Mar., 31 Mar.

Lucky Days: 12 Mar, 24 Mar.
Misfortune Days: 9 Mar, 21 Mar.
Bad Days: 6 Mar, 18 Mar., 30 Mar.

Month 3 in the Rabbit Year (6 Apr 23 - 5 May 23)
This month, auspicious stars appear in the house of destiny and are influenced by allied months. As a result, problems and obstacles will be resolved, whether they are work-related or financial. This is not a smooth rhythm. You also have an adult assisting you to ensure that the work runs smoothly. As a result, you should summarize previous problems and errors as a lesson to quickly adjust some plans to fit and create a backup plan to prevent problems from occurring later in the plans or projects that you have planned. You can do it this month because there are auspicious stars to send your way, and you should increase your prosperity.

In terms of salary, this will provide a substantial income, but you must be diligent to continuously develop yourself. Because the trade will be encouraged to advance if you work hard this month. You will also make a substantial amount of money. So, even if tired, the wealth gained is worth it.

The auspicious power is coming this month for the family, so it's a good time to take the family members on a long vacation or go out to make merit and make merit together to enhance good auspicious energy. Furthermore, during this time, you will be required to purchase expensive property for the house.

Moi takes warm care of each other during this period of love. This will be a lucky time for some of you. For a proposal, engagement, or marriage

Your health is good, but don't take it for granted. You should continue to exercise every day.

Support Days: 4 Apr., 8 Apr., 12 Apr., 16 Apr., 20 Apr., 24 Apr., 28 Apr.
Lucky Days: 5 Apr., 17 Apr., 29 Apr.
Misfortune Days: 2 Apr., 14 Apr., 26 Apr.

Bad Days: 11 Apr., 23 Apr.

Month 4 in the Rabbit Year (6 May 23 - 5 Jun 23)
Destiny's path has been plagued by monsoons this month, causing his fate to plummet. Businesses and commerce will face numerous challenges and trials. There are numerous challenges in store for you. As a result, you must carefully consider each step before taking any action. Allowing the little dots to pass will cause problems later. Management At this stage, you will encounter story conflicts. It is preferable to avoid than to react or crash.

The salary aspect is not favorable; you will receive less, pay more, and have a reason to lose money in unexpected circumstances. You should also avoid gambling and investing in businesses that are illegal in your country.

During this time, you should pay special attention to the health of your family members and unexpected accidents.

Lack of moisture in love is caused by both parties not having enough time for each other to continue making love. Small points can easily become larger due to misunderstandings, which you may be able to resolve by continuing to call or employing other technologies to assist.

Accidental injuries should be avoided in terms of physical health. Gum bleeding is possible.

Seats were unkind to relatives and friends, and there were no people to assist.

In terms of forming joint ventures, starting a new job, and investing in various fields, this is not a good time. You should first refrain.

Support Days: 2 May., 6 May., 10 May., 14 May., 18 May., 22 May., 26 May., and 30 May.
Lucky Days: 11 May., 23 May.
Misfortune Days: 8 May., 20 May.
Bad Days: 5 May., 17 May., 29 May.

Month 5 in the Rabbit Year (6 Jun 23 - 6 Jul 23)
This month's destiny criterion has passed the clash and has begun to move in a more positive direction. However, the challenges remain. As a result, anything that you should be able to solve decisively should be dealt with as soon as possible rather than leaving it as clay masking a pig's tail. by first addressing the critical points, then preparing the necessary factors, and finally addressing other critical problems Wait for an advantageous moment, then proceed fully.

This salary horoscope indicates a high level of direct cash flow. There will be a lot of risk with the money expected from fortune. However, you should exercise caution when it comes to spending. Should put money aside for revolving when there is a financial crisis.

There is a direction of progress in the field of work, and being very diligent will result in you receiving a lot as well as finding patrons to help support you. Supervisors and colleagues both contribute to the smooth operation of the work.

But the most important thing to remember is that you must know how to care for your colleagues if there is a small gift for an important occasion to show kindness. It will make things go more smoothly.

This month brings peace, love, and harmony to the family.

When it comes to love, it's like having an angel holding you up because no matter what you say or do, they all seem to agree. However, in the case of poor health, the evil star is aimed at the health base. As a result, you should be cautious of accidents on the road. Be cautious of food poisoning.

During this time, relatives and friends are a great source of comfort.

Support Days: 3 Jun., 7 Jun., 11 Jun., 15 Jun., 19 Jun., 23 Jun., 27 Jun.
Lucky Days: 4 Jun., 16 Jun., 28 Jun.
Misfortune Days: 1 Jun., 13 Jun., 25 Jun.
Bad Days: 10 Jun., 22 Jun.

Month 6 in the Rabbit Year (7 Jul 23 - 7 Aug 23)
This month's destiny criteria have performed better than the previous month's. Problems and obstacles in the outstanding work will be identified with supporters and fixed as soon as possible. Even when interpersonal conflicts do not erupt violently, they create underwater waves.

This month, you should focus on increasing understanding, reducing stress, and utilizing synergies. Be kind to everyone and be fair to everyone. It is critical to understand how to care for your coworkers, especially if you have a small gift for a special occasion. Everything will run more smoothly as a result. It also aids in the dispersal of underwater waves in another way.

In terms of pay, this is mediocre in terms of measuring luck, and high-risk floating fortunes. As a result, it should be avoided before it is safe, and you should be wary of unforeseen current expenditures piling up, causing your liquidity to become stuck. As a result, to have flexible working capital, unnecessary expenditures should be reduced first.

The family is at peace once more, and there may be some fortunate events taking place at home.

This month will bring love to singles. However, there will be competitors to contend with. As a result, you should maintain your cool.

However, be cautious of food poisoning. Be on the lookout for infectious diseases and other ailments to request.

This month is favorable for family and friends. You'll find people to assist you.

You can invest, but you must exercise extreme caution.

Support Days: 1 Jul., 5 Jul., 9 Jul., 13 Jul., 17 Jul., 21 Jul., 25 Jul., 29 Jul.
Lucky Days: 10 Jul., 22 Jul.
Misfortune Days: 7 Jul., 19 Jul., 31 Jul.
Bad Days: 4 Jul., 16 Jul., 28 Jul.

Month 7 in the Rabbit Year (8 Aug 23 - 7 Sep 23)
Your destiny has changed this month if you were born in the year of the Monkey. Businesses and trades can work together in perfect harmony, and progress will be visible. However, the conflict has not been fully resolved.

This month, here's what you should do. A broad vision is required in business. Investigate the market's future and the product's popularity trend. If the old channel is perfect this month, you still have a chance to penetrate the market and open up new channels, which will always help you to make your pioneering success. There will be a rhythm for those of you who work regularly to demonstrate your abilities to the commander and those in the vicinity.

On the plus side, this salary has a usable inflow of income. However, you must exercise caution when it comes to spending. Don't enjoy spending so much that your wallet runs dry before the end of the month. There will be a part of luck fluke and fortune floating around during this period. But be careful not to be greedy. Otherwise, they will be caught in a trap until they have to pay out.

For a peaceful family, this could be an expensive house purchase or a large feast. More good news.

There will be people on the love side to help share and care for the heart. As a result, you must divide your time between watering and fertilizing the love plant for it to grow. Don't allow a third hand to enter the picture and cause a schism in your love life.

There will be some illnesses and illnesses during this period if you are in good health. But you shouldn't be too concerned.

People will come to help and advice relatives and friends as they go through the crisis, and they will have the opportunity to work together. Invest in new and interesting businesses together.

Support Days: 2 Aug., 6 Aug., 10 Aug., 14 Aug.,
18 Aug., 22 Aug., 26 Aug., 30 Aug.
Lucky Days: 3 Aug., 15 Aug., 27 Aug.
Misfortune Days: 12 Aug., 24 Aug.
Bad Days: 9 Aug., 21 Aug.

Month 8 in the Rabbit Year (8 Sep 23 - 7 Oct 23)

This month's destiny will include both good and bad aspects. One thing to keep in mind is to keep a close eye on the liquidity of working capital. Allowing the red to stick with a crisis and then lobbying to fix it will result in you losing credibility. Furthermore, it is best to avoid investing in high-risk, large-capitalized companies.

During this stage of your job, you should stay on top of market trends and changes in factors beyond your control. To minimize potential problems, they must be flexible and adaptable to their business.

The most important thing you should do now is your best. Avoid causing conflicts with close friends and colleagues. Otherwise, they may be left alone and forced to solve problems on their own. This period of trade work, despite its obstacles and conflicts. But if you have good intentions, nothing is beyond your reach.

This salary horoscope has been harmed. All risks should be avoided because the evil stars Humpty and Dao Ngwe Sua are aiming for the moon base. Gambling, gambling, doing business that is illegal and prohibits others from borrowing money or signing guarantees.

The family is still at peace, loving each other, and reconciling.

As for love, it is bright, sweet, loving, and caring. Some couples may have auspicious events or new members to make you happy.

However, in poor health, you must exercise extreme caution to avoid accidents.

For family and friends Collaboration and investment are both undesirable. You must still skip the period first.

Support Days: 3 Sep, 7 Sep., 11 Sep, 15 Sep, 19 Sep., 23 Sep., 27 Sep.
Lucky Days: 8 Sep, 20 Sep.
Misfortune Days: 5 Sep, 17 Sep., 29 Sep.
Bad Days: 2 Sep, 14 Sep., 26 Sep.

Month 9 in the Rabbit Year (8 Oct 23 - 6 Nov 23)

Your fate criteria This month has returned to a downward trend. Things that used to run smoothly will come to a halt.

The most important thing is to ask you to remain calm and calm. Activities that require a great deal of responsibility. Before making a decision, seek the advice of an adult. Including a variety of problems and roadblocks. If you are unsure, seek advice from someone knowledgeable. They should also take care of their working capital.

This salary fate is not favorable. Income is consistent, but expenditure per queue is extremely high. There is also a surprising leak point. Please be mindful of how you manage the money in your pocket during this time.

Always carefully examine the accounts that provide long-term credit. Be wary of bad debts. You should not lend money to others if your financial star is unlucky. Do not use the word "guarantee" to anyone. Avoid gambling, gambling, speculation, and vices in general.

Meet people who are challenging in your field of work. As a result, you must assign the right people to the job and understand how to manage your emotions. You should not go out with your customers or contacts. To keep the customer base and prevent them from leaving.

For the family who still loves and reconciles well, providing you with some solace.

However, there will be disagreements in the love department. As a result, avoid getting involved in the problems of your friends and family at this time. To avoid problems, it is best to avoid going to entertainment venues.

This is a bad time for your health. Keep an eye out for gastritis. Inflammatory bowel disease, heart disease, food poisoning, and automobile accidents.

Support Days: 1 Oct., 5 Oct., 9 Oct., 13 Oct., 17 Oct., 21 Oct., 25 Oct., 29 Oct.
Lucky Days: 2 Oct., 14 Oct., 26 Oct.
Misfortune Days: 11 Oct., 23 Oct.
Bad Days: 8 Oct., 20 Oct.

Month 10 in the Rabbit Year (7 Nov 23 - 6 Dec 23)
The path of destiny for this month has returned to the shadows. As "Kuo Hu" (Lord of the Lawsuit) orbits to destroy the House of Destiny, be wary of tax evasion or the purchase of counterfeit goods. The law may cause you to lose your property or cause trouble if you lobby for the defense of allegations, and you must be cautious of being held liable without cause.

This month, you should avoid engaging in any illegal activities at all costs. Do not get involved in other people's problems.

In terms of commercial work, you must also be cautious of work conflicts. Avoid conflicts with other people's interests by negotiating leniently and sharing allocations. It will not be worth it to give in to a dispute.

In terms of pay, there is still the issue of misplacing property and incurring unending petty expenses. As a result, reducing some of your cravings and abandoning some of your more enterprising habits will provide you with a lot more liquidity. This month, you must avoid being greedy because it will result in more losses.

This month is a good time to strengthen singles' relationships. In a romantic confession. There will be a criterion for those who have been in a relationship for a while to agree to ring the wedding bell during this period.

In terms of overall health, high blood pressure should be avoided, as should grilled food, and accidents while traveling should be avoided.

Relatives, friends, and investments are all bad ideas.

Support Days: 2 Nov., 6 Nov., 10 Nov., 14 Nov., 18 Nov., 22 Nov., 26 Nov., 30 Nov.
Lucky Days: 7 Nov., 19 Nov.
Misfortune Days: 4 Nov., 16 Nov., 28 Nov.
Bad Days: 1 Nov., 13 Nov., 25 Nov.

Month 11 in the Rabbit Year (7 Dec 23 - 5 Jan 24)

This month, your fate criterion was born in the year of the Monkey. Because we are entering the month of the alliance and receiving auspicious power from the auspicious stars shining, the obstacles of previous problems are gradually dissolving. Work-related activities, including business, will thrive. As a result, you should seize this fantastic opportunity to showcase your skills. Build your work and make your sales thrive and multiply so that the returns that come back will make you feel refreshed, relieved, and replaced after the previous months of adversity.

This salary fortune is considered a stroke of luck. Whether it is regular income, fortune, float, or success in earning extra income through other channels, Revenue appears to have increased sequentially. However, one must be cautious about spending, which must be carefully monitored.

The members of a peaceful family have a good relationship and help each other.

Close relatives and friends are all there for one another. If you consider investing together, you will have the opportunity to receive excellent returns.

Love has been shining brightly for the past month. But please don't be a good start and a soft finish. Maintaining good deeds will cause things to change in the way you think.

If you are in good health during this time, be wary of the stomach and intestinal issues. Those with the congenital disease should be cautious of reoccurring diseases. Maintain the strength and immunity of both your body and mind. And another month to be cautious of car accidents while traveling.

Support Days: 4 Dec., 8 Dec., 12 Dec., 16 Dec., 20 Dec., 24 Dec., 28 Dec.

Lucky Days: 2 Dec., 14 Dec., 26 Dec.
Misfortune Days: 1 Dec., 13 Dec., 25 Dec.
Bad Days: 7 Dec., 19 Dec., 31 Dec.

Amulet for The Year of the Monkey
"Triratana Bodhisattva"
Those born in the Monkey year this year
should create and worship sacred objects.
Place "Phra Triratana Bodhisattva" on your
desk or cash desk to ask for mercy from the
three gods to enhance the auspicious things to
make the results manifest. There has been
advancement and success. filled with infinite
wealth and a happy family, but prosperity
comes to the fate

(Note: The final text of your life cycle can be
used to determine the direction in which
sacred objects should be established.)

Chapter one of the Department of Advanced
Feng Shui discusses the gods who will descend
to reside in the yearly mikeng (destiny house),
who are the gods who can bring both good and
bad to the fate of that year. When this is the
case, worshiping to increase your luck with
the gods who come down to reside in the same
year of your birth is thought to be the best and
most affecting you to rely on the gods' prestige

to help protect you. There was some misfortune to be alleviated as his destiny fell. At the same time, I'd like to wish you blessings to help inspire the smooth running of your business as you seek to bring prosperity and prosperity to yourself and your family.

Sim is the sign of those born in the Year of the Monkey or Mi Keng (House of Destiny). Whatever work you take on this year, It appears to be silver and gold in color. To advance your work, you should broaden your society. However, because there are so many unlucky constellations in the horoscope. This year, you have the criteria to easily argue with anyone. As a result, I ask that you be mindful and stand tall. Please be cautious in your decisions regarding work and finances. Be wary of being duped or scammed, as well as of lawsuits and the safety of family members. The minor or his family will cause pain and damage. The rough side of love is full of stumbling blocks. It will be difficult to move on if you remain stubborn in your thoughts. Food hygiene is important for health, and digestive system inflammation should be avoided. If you want to avoid disasters, you should make and wear amulets. "Phra Triratana Bodhisattva" to ask the three gods for the power of prestige to help dispel misfortunes, bring good fortune, and promote prosperity and increase in any business, there are all who help and patronize to be smooth and successful.

The main Buddha image in the middle of his left is "Phra Triratana Bodhisattva" (Sampa Devi), which includes three "Phra Avalokitesvara Bodhisattvas." "Phra Bodhisattva Manjusri" (Bun Chu Phosak), the one on his right side who excels in wisdom. "Phra Bodhisattva Samatphat" (Pow Iang Phosak), the one who excels in the beauty of morality; all three are regarded as great Bodhisattvas with a strong desire to relieve animal suffering. As a result, summoning "Phra Triratana Bodhisattva" set up in a house or office will contribute to receiving mercy from the three gods from obstacles, thorns, and misfortunes. Increased good fortune Work duties and business transactions run smoothly and as planned.

Those born in the Year of the Monkey should also wear auspicious pendants. You can wear "Phra Triratana Bodhisattva" around your neck or carry it with you when traveling both near and far. To fill your destiny with auspicious wealth, prosperity, and advancement in both business and work. A happy family all year results in greater efficiency and productivity, faster than ever before.

Good Direction: Northwest, Southeast, and Southwest
Bad Direction: Northeast
Lucky Colors: White, Yellow, Gold, and Blue.
Lucky Times: 9.00 – 10.59, 15.00 – 16.59, 23.00 – 00.59.
Bad Times: 03.00 – 04.59, 21.00 – 22.59.

Good Luck For 2023